THE OUTSIDER
FILMMAKER

START YOUR FILM WITHOUT FUNDING

ANTHONY R. FERRARO

First published in 2023

ISBN: 979-8-218-26297-6

Printed in the United States of America

This book is dedicated to my parents, Geraldine and Anthony, for their unwavering support and encouragement.

TABLE OF CONTENTS

INTRODUCTION

My journey as an outsider filmmaker has been filled with diverse experiences, challenges, and breakthroughs. Coming from a theater background and finding myself at the dawn of the digital filmmaking revolution, I left the theatre armed only with a passion for storytelling to start my filmmaking journey.

Inspired by the Dogme 95 movement, founded by Lars von Trier and Thomas Vinterberg, I fully embraced the movement's emphasis on contemporary storytelling and the unwavering priority given to authentic acting, triumphing over the formidable technical and financial obstacles commonly encountered in conventional filmmaking. The Dogme 95 movement, with its rebellious spirit akin to punk rock, had a profound impact on permitting me to try my hand at filmmaking. I was particularly drawn to a few of its rules that liberated me creatively—shooting exclusively on location without bringing in props or sets; never separating sound from images; embracing hand-held camera work and adhering to the use of natural lighting by rejecting special lighting or filters. These rules, rather than being a mere checklist, became guiding principles that removed all my imagined boundaries of filmmaking and inspired me to try my hand at it.

It is true that being an outsider filmmaker has its obstacles—limited funding, a lack of industry connections, and navigating established norms. However, it was these very challenges that fueled my determination to forge my own path and tell stories that resonated with audiences. I went on to make two feature films loosely following those guidelines and was at the beginning of the post-Dogme 95 movement that would become known in the States as mumblecore.

Through exploration of this style of filmmaking, I discovered the possibilities of repeated attempts at storytelling. Admittedly, my early attempts, while passionate and sometimes unique and exciting, lacked well-structured narratives that could hold an audience's attention. However, two key factors laid out my pathway to creative expression and growth. The first, was to embrace unconventional funding methods. I would not have evolved as a filmmaker and storyteller if I had spent five years trying to raise money for a single project instead of making five films within that time. The second: to always prioritize captivating narratives. For this, I found it incredibly helpful to embrace various storytelling frameworks, such as Freytag's Pyramid, The Hero's Journey, Three Act Structure, Dan Harmon's Story Circle, Fichtean Curve, Save the

Cat Beat Sheet, and Seven-Point Story Structure. These narrative blueprints have enriched my craft and provided a solid foundation for creating compelling and resonant stories. (See chapter 2.)

My appreciation for simplicity and understanding of budget constraints became my strength. Focused storytelling and resourceful filmmaking created engaging experiences for the audience. I've written and directed over a dozen films, gaining recognition and millions of views on streaming platforms. Through my YouTube channel, I share what I've learned and the new ideas I'm currently exploring.

As an outsider filmmaker, my dedication is fueled by a genuine love for storytelling. While financial success would be welcomed, my priority remains in the art itself. I acknowledge the challenges outsiders face in obtaining opportunities and emphasize the need to find a way forward. I want to be transparent and assure you that I'm not trying to promote lofty ideals of art. My motivation is rooted in my love for making movies and telling stories. The best advice I ever received was, "The cavalry is not coming." If you are waiting for someone to make your dreams come true… Guess what! They're not coming.

My Aims in Writing This Book

Funds to bring your movie or series idea to life can feel like a distant dream, and finding someone willing to invest can seem impossible. It's common to fear the temptation of relying on credit cards or to avoid the uncomfortable prospect of asking friends and family for financial support. However, I want you to know that you're not alone in this journey. I've encountered these hurdles and developed the practical approach set out in this guide.

I call it the *Momentum Budget*. Through it, you'll take charge of your project and deal with financial obstacles without depending on external investors to get things started. It is rooted in my own experiences and the valuable lessons I've learned along the way. I'll share practical strategies, proven techniques, and authentic insights to empower you in making your movie or series on a limited budget. It's time to bring your creative vision to life and transform your idea into a reality. We'll navigate the challenges and embark on this exciting filmmaking adventure with authenticity and determination.

Let's clarify something right from the start: this is not a masterclass on industry practices or the standard path to success. Instead, I focus on showing you how to bring your ideas to life and make your film a reality. The Momentum Budget is about commitment and setting achievable goals, regardless of your financial limitations.

In the chapters that follow we will be breaking the Momentum Budget down into four key phases:

1. The Free Phase
2. The Friend Phase
3. The Finance Phase
4. The Finishing Phase

This DIY approach may seem overwhelming to some and overly simple to others. However, for those desiring to bring a movie idea to life, the Momentum Budget can be your path forward. It won't be easy, comfortable, or glamorous, but it will get your film made. It's a long game. Staying committed to and focused on the end goal is essential.

The Outsider Filmmaker

CHAPTER ONE
DEFINITIONS

Let's start by laying the groundwork for this simple, practical filmmaking guide. In this chapter, we will explore fundamental concepts such as the "Momentum Budget" and "The Four F's" (Free, Friends, Finance, and Finish) to guide you through various project phases. Understanding these essential elements is crucial to unlocking the book's practical and straightforward approach. By addressing this information at the beginning, you can immediately gain useful and actionable insights to embark on your filmmaking journey.

In addition, I will be clear about the essence of DIY Filmmaking as it applies to this book, empowering you to overcome challenges and bring your creative vision to life. These definitions form a solid foundation for comprehending the book's approach, making it easier to navigate the complexities of starting a film project without funding in place.

The "Momentum Budget"

The *Momentum Budget* is a commitment to a series of goals that *progressively* move your project forward, gaining traction and propulsion with each step. It starts with primary goals that only cost your time, then moves on to collaboration goals, and finally incorporates goals that require funding. It recognizes that filmmaking can be challenging, especially when money is scarce, but it provides a practical and effective framework to make things happen. Rather than allowing obstacles to discourage or hinder progress, the Momentum Budget offers a practical and effective framework for taking that first step through a philosophy that emphasizes resourcefulness, creativity, and collaboration; whereby, instead of solely relying on money, you explore alternative solutions and leverage the skills and talents of your team. It encourages you to think outside the box, finding innovative ways to achieve your desired results.

At its core, the Momentum Budget is about utilizing the resources you have at your disposal, such as your time, creativity, and the support of others. Rather than being discouraged by financial limitations, it encourages you to focus on what you can do and to take action. The key is to create a sense of forward momentum, gradually propelling your vision from the realm of ideas into tangible reality. By breaking down your larger objectives into smaller, actionable steps, you can make steady progress even with limited financial means. Setting goals and breaking them down into manageable steps creates a sense of direction and purpose.

Beyond that, this guide is a strategic approach that transforms challenges into opportunities. It encourages you to view constraints as catalysts for creativity and innovation, empowering you to find innovative solutions and workarounds. By embracing this framework, you can navigate the complexities of filmmaking with determination, resilience, and a steadfast commitment to making your vision a reality, regardless of the financial limitations you may encounter.

Remember, it is not about boasting or seeking validation. It's a DIY guide for those who are driven, committed, and willing to take the necessary steps. With the right mindset, dedication, and a committed team, you can overcome financial barriers and bring your story to the screen. The momentum budget approach may be different from the conventional, but it's a viable option for those who are passionate and dedicated to getting their projects done.

The "Four F's"

The *Four F's* – *Free, Friends, Finance,* and *Finish* – provide a memorable and practical framework for navigating the challenges of low-budget filmmaking. Each F represents a distinct phase in the momentum budget process, symbolizing the progression from initial ideation to the completion of your project.

The first phase, the *Free Phase*, emphasizes investing time and commitment. It's about dedicating yourself to the creative process, writing the script, and gathering support materials without financial constraints. Though it may require significant effort, this phase sets the foundation for your film and establishes the momentum needed to move forward.

Next comes the *Friends Phase*, where you assemble your core team and collaborate closely with them. Regular meetings and managing expectations are vital components of this phase. It may involve small gestures like hosting meetings at your home, providing meals, and nurturing a supportive environment. Building strong relationships and treating your team members with respect fosters a sense of camaraderie and fuels the collaborative spirit.

I want to pause before the next phase... I believe in being straightforward and transparent, so here's the deal: the real power of the "momentum approach" *starts with these first two phases.*

If you begin by focusing as so many do on the third F, Finance, you can get stuck in a never-ending cycle of pitching projects and not making them. However, when you commit to the writing in the Free Phase and involve others during the Friend Phase, the Finance Phase becomes another bump in the road, something you need to roll over no matter how bumpy, rather than a barrier that stops you in your tracks. So let's move onto it...

The *Finance Phase* introduces the reality of budget considerations. Determining your budget, exploring funding options, and setting a clear time frame for raising funds become the focal points. Though it may be a daunting task, the momentum gained from the previous phases helps propel you forward. By aligning your financial goals with the project's vision, you create a roadmap for success.

Finally, the *Finish Phase* signifies the home stretch of your filmmaking journey. It involves scheduling shooting dates, creating post-production schedules, and setting deadlines. This phase is where the culmination of your efforts comes to fruition as you work diligently to complete your film and aim for festival submissions and streaming opportunities. The sense of urgency and determination to meet deadlines becomes paramount.

While the *Four F's* may appear corny, their simplicity and memorability make them practical tools for organizing and conceptualizing your filmmaking process. They serve as guideposts along the journey, reminding you of the elements essential to making your film dream a reality. Embracing the *Four F's* with a dash of self-awareness can help you stay focused, motivated, and prepared to overcome the challenges that come your way.

DIY Filmmaking

When people mention "DIY filmmaking," it's often associated with low-budget projects or indie films. However, "DIY" encompasses much more than a mere label for affordability. DIY filmmaking is a mindset, an approach that emphasizes the process of doing things yourself and taking control of your creative vision. You ignore at your peril the "Y" in DIY, which stands for Yourself and not for a Yeah that's practically free and easy.

Understanding the DIY Mentality

At its core, the DIY mentality in filmmaking is about being resourceful, resilient, and willing to put in the hard work. DIY filmmakers often rely on online resources, tutorials, and communities to acquire the necessary knowledge and skills. Rather than waiting for someone else to make things happen, they take the initiative to learn, experiment, and create.

The Power of Online Resources

One of the most remarkable aspects of DIY filmmaking in the modern era is the wealth of online resources available to aspiring filmmakers. Websites, forums, and video platforms provide access to tutorials, guides, and discussions on various aspects of filmmaking, from scriptwriting to cinematography, editing, and distribution. These resources offer invaluable insights, techniques, and practical tips shared by experienced filmmakers, enabling newcomers to learn and grow in their craft.

The Realities of DIY Filmmaking

While the accessibility of online resources is undoubtedly beneficial, it's essential to recognize the realities of DIY filmmaking. It requires time, dedication, and a willingness to learn and adapt. DIY filmmakers often take on multiple roles, from writing and directing to producing, cinematography, editing, and beyond. They become a one-person production team, wearing different hats throughout the filmmaking process.

The Challenges and Rewards

DIY filmmaking comes with its fair share of challenges. Limited budgets, equipment constraints, and a lack of professional experience can present obstacles. By embracing any limitations and finding inventive solutions, DIY filmmakers can create unique and compelling works of art. The sense of accomplishment and the ability to see your creative vision come to life is among the most rewarding aspects of DIY filmmaking.

The Importance of Collaboration

Although DIY filmmaking often involves working independently, collaboration remains a crucial element. Forming partnerships, networking with like-minded individuals, and seeking support from the filmmaking community can significantly enhance your DIY journey. Collaborators can bring complementary skills, fresh perspectives, and added expertise to your project, elevating its overall quality and impact.

Embracing the DIY Spirit

Ultimately, the essence of DIY filmmaking lies in embracing the spirit of self-reliance, resourcefulness, and determination. It's about owning your ideas and making them a reality, regardless of financial limitations or industry barriers. DIY filmmaking is not a shortcut or an easy path to success. It requires passion, perseverance, and a willingness to learn, adapt, and grow as a filmmaker.

The Empowering Journey of DIY Filmmaking

DIY filmmaking is an empowering journey that enables aspiring filmmakers to overcome obstacles, unleash their creativity, and bring their ideas to life. By embracing the DIY mentality and utilizing the vast array of online resources available, you can acquire the knowledge and skills needed to navigate the complexities of the filmmaking process. While DIY filmmaking may be challenging, it offers a unique avenue for self-expression, personal growth, and making your film a reality.

Anthony Ferraro

CHAPTER TWO
THE FREE PHASE

The first step of the Momentum Budget is the Free Phase—a phase that costs little to no money but demands a considerable investment of time and dedication. During this phase, we emphasize the importance of looking ahead and making a firm commitment to progress, avoiding stagnation in the planning stage. Writing and refining the script, along with creating support materials, carry no financial burden but require your passionate commitment. This zero-cost investment of time allows you to refine your ideas and unleash your creativity, providing a solid groundwork for the subsequent phases of your filmmaking adventure.

It's like laying the first bricks of a sturdy structure, creating a solid platform for what comes next. As you move forward, you'll find yourself building upon this groundwork, leveraging your dedication and creativity, and progressing step by step towards bringing your film to life. This phase embodies the spirit of resourcefulness, determination, and ingenuity—essential traits that will carry you through the journey ahead.

Igniting Momentum

Getting started simply requires a devoted investment of time, not monetary means. Now is the time to firmly commit to moving ahead and steer clear of getting bogged down in the planning of how you'd do things if you did, in fact, have a decent budget (you don't). Though it demands considerable time, surging forward is the spark to igniting momentum. It's about laying the groundwork, step by step, to pave your way to a road that has been off-limits until now.

Writing, Refining, and Creating Support Materials

The primary objective of the Free Phase is to write the script, refine it, and create support materials that will shape the foundation of your project. As a DIY filmmaker, being the writer and director allows you to take control of various aspects of the production process. You'll be involved in crafting the story, developing characters, and ensuring your creative vision remains intact.

Harnessing Creative Tools

This is a phase in which it's beneficial to leverage any creative tools or skills you possess. For those who can draw, creating storyboards and concept art can aid in visualizing key scenes and sequences. Even if drawing isn't your forte, you can still gather reference materials from the internet. Collecting images related to color palettes, landscapes, clothing, and character types helps establish a visual framework for your project.

Set a Date for a Reading

Setting a specific date for a group read-through serves as a motivating force to complete the script and move the project forward. The date needs to be scheduled to fall within the Friend Phase, when you will have help bringing your script to life through a reading. Through it, you will gain valuable insights into its strengths and weaknesses and have an opportunity to engage with potential collaborators early on and generate enthusiasm for the project.

In today's digital age, the prevalence of video conferencing tools has made organizing table reads even more accessible and convenient. With the ability to connect participants from different locations, virtual table reads eliminate geographical barriers and facilitate collaboration, even when physical gatherings are not feasible. This opens up new possibilities for zero-budget or low-budget projects, allowing them to benefit from the same script development practices as higher-budget productions.

The Power of the Free Phase

This phase of the Momentum Budget represents the initial investment of time and creative energy in your filmmaking journey.

By committing to writing, refining the script, creating support materials, and setting a date for a reading, you set wheels in motion and create a sense of momentum. The free phase establishes a strong foundation for your project, paving the way for collaboration and growth.

Script Writing and Refinement

Unleashing the Power of Storytelling is the first step on your filmmaking journey. As you write the first page of your script, you embark on the crucial process of script writing and refinement, which holds the key to bringing your film project to life.

The Craft of Script Writing

Scriptwriting is crafting a narrative that captivates audiences and brings characters to life on the screen. It involves creating a structured blueprint that guides the visual, auditory, and emotional elements of your film. As a beginner, understanding the fundamentals of script writing is essential for effectively communicating your ideas and engaging viewers.

Writing a Cohesive Story

A well-crafted script begins with a strong foundation in storytelling. It is the vehicle through which you convey your themes, characters, and the journey they undertake. Using various storytelling techniques and frameworks, you can create a cohesive and compelling narrative that resonates with your audience. On a practical level, these storytelling techniques become powerful tools that enhance your creative process and help you navigate the complexities of scriptwriting. Crafting your story within a framework provides clear direction and structure, preventing you from getting lost in the vast expanse of ideas. With a roadmap, you can confidently move from the beginning to the middle and the end, seamlessly weaving your narrative together.

Story Structures

In this book, emphasis is placed on the importance of structure for storytelling without delving into intricate writing process details. Abundant research exists on various narrative techniques and frameworks. A solid system forms a robust foundation for crafting compelling, impactful stories that resonate with audiences.

Start by exploring the seven widely recognized and time-tested story structures that have captivated audiences throughout history. From Freytag's Pyramid, which introduces rising tension and a climactic resolution, to the renowned Hero's Journey, taking protagonists on transformative quests, each structure deploys these fundamental components uniquely and compellingly. The Three Act Structure, Dan Harmon's Story Circle, Fichtean Curve, Save the Cat Beat Sheet, and the Seven-Point Story Structure are prominent methods to craft engaging and emotionally resonant tales. By acquainting yourself with these narrative blueprints, you can hone your craft, making your storytelling more captivating to an audience.

Utilizing Online Resources

The same is true here as it was for Phase One: in today's digital age, aspiring filmmakers have a wealth of online resources to aid in scriptwriting. From screenwriting software and A.I. assistance to online tutorials and forums, these resources offer valuable insights, tips, and techniques to help you develop your script. Websites and communities dedicated to screenwriting can provide guidance on structure, dialogue, character development, and more.

A Note on Writing With A.I.

While A.I. has significantly improved its ability to assist and even write for you, I advise against relying on it for your first project. Personally, I have found it to be a powerful and valuable tool, but it should be seen as just that—a tool. I have developed my technique and storytelling style over the past two decades. Recently I have begun incorporating A.I. as an assistant in my creative process. If this is your first script, I strongly recommend resisting the urge to use A.I. I asked *ChatGPT* for its perspective on writing a screenplay with AI, and here's its response:

A.I.'s Thoughts on the Subject

"As an AI language model, I don't possess personal thoughts, opinions, or subjective experiences. I can provide information and generate responses based on patterns and examples from the data I've been trained on. Regarding writing a screenplay with AI, it can be an intriguing and powerful tool to assist in the creative process. AI can help with generating ideas, enhancing efficiency, and providing alternative perspectives. However, it's essential to remember that AI-generated content should be approached with critical thinking and human oversight. Ultimately, the decision to use AI in screenwriting is subjective and depends on individual preferences and goals."

The Zero-Cost Investment – Time

One of the remarkable aspects of scriptwriting is that it requires no monetary investment; only your time and dedication. The way you choose to spend this time in the initial stages will ultimately be reflected in the end result. By committing to the Free Phase of the Momentum Budget, you invest your time in writing the script, creating support materials, and organizing a reading. This phase sets the groundwork for your project and allows you to refine your ideas without any financial burden. The zero-cost nature of script writing allows you to channel your passion and unleash your creativity, setting the stage for the subsequent phases of your filmmaking adventure.

Refining Your Script

The process of script refinement is an ongoing journey. As you write and receive feedback, you can refine and enhance your script. It involves revisiting and strengthening your story, improving dialogue, fine-tuning character arcs, and ensuring narrative coherence. Seeking feedback from trusted peers or participating in script workshops can provide valuable insights and perspectives to help you refine your work, as will your read-through in the next phase.

Creating Support Materials

As well as the mood boards and drawings already mentioned, it is valuable to gather objects and pieces of clothing that can be used in your film or serve as visual aids to communicate your vision to collaborators effectively. This curated collection of items helps bring your ideas to life in a tangible way. Additionally, immerse yourself in films that inspire you visually. Capture screenshots of visually impactful moments. Explore scenes and lighting looks that align with your creative vision. These cinematic references act as a springboard, igniting your imagination and facilitating effective communication of your ideas to others involved in the project.

Considering Time Investment

In my twenties, while working as a bartender in NYC, I had an older colleague, we'll call him Bob, who went above and beyond his job responsibilities. Despite not being a manager, he voluntarily arrived early to organize schedules and stock inventory. He went out of his way to make all the patrons feel like this was their place. Intrigued, I asked him one day why he put in all that extra effort. He responded sincerely and thoughtfully, explaining that he couldn't invest money to get ahead in life since he lived paycheck to paycheck. However, he realized that he could invest his time to get ahead. His words didn't resonate strongly with me then, as I was eager to move on with my life. Fast forward ten years later, when I revisited the bar during a visit to NYC, I discovered that Bob had become the establishment's co-owner. Over time, the original bar owner recognized that the establishment's success was directly attributed to Bob's dedicated efforts. It was a sound business decision to make Bob his partner. Hearing Bob converse with the customers and observing his success, the concept of investing time became etched in my mind. From that point onward, I followed his example every single day.

The Free Phase – Action Points

- Commit to progress and avoid getting stuck in the planning stage.

- Embrace the free phase to invest time in your filmmaking journey.

- Write and continuously refine your script as the writer-director.

- Gather objects, clothing, and online references as visual aids.

- Study visually inspiring films and capture impactful screenshots.

- Set a date for a script reading.

- Write a script with a clear structure, utilizing storytelling techniques and frameworks.

- Identify objects and clothing aligned with your film's vision.

- Create a mood board or lookbook for visualization.

- Reflect on feedback, revise, and refine the script.

- Research story structures:
Freytag's Pyramid
The Hero's Journey
Three Act Structure
Dan Harmon's Story Circle
Fichtean Curve
Save the Cat Beat Sheet
Seven-Point Story Structure

CHAPTER THREE
THE FRIEND PHASE

The Friend Phase is a critical stage in your filmmaking journey where collaboration and momentum take center stage. The goals and strategies involved in this phase include:

- gathering your core team
- establishing regular meetings
- effectively managing expectations

As you navigate the challenges of low-budget filmmaking, the Friend Phase sets the foundation for productive collaboration and propels your project forward.

Additionally, the Friend Phase prompts you to think aloud about your project. It becomes essential to have open discussions with your collaborators about what is realistic within your DIY, low-budget approach. Assessing the script's feasibility and making adjustments is crucial. For example, if your script involves multiple locations, you may need to consolidate them into a more manageable number. If a scene is set in a busy mall, consider adapting it to a local grocery store. These decisions set the stage for the next phase, where you will delve into the financial aspect of your project.

Remember, the Friend Phase is an opportunity to harness the collective creativity and dedication of your team. By fostering collaboration, respecting one another, and engaging in open discussions, you will navigate the challenges ahead and build the necessary momentum to bring your filmmaking aspirations to life. In embracing collaboration and realistic planning, the Friend Phase sets the stage for the next chapter, where you will dive into the intricacies of financing your project.

Gathering Your Core Team

One of the primary objectives is to assemble your core team. Like starting a band, having a cohesive and dedicated group of individuals is essential for success.

The Ideal Core Team

To kickstart your project, it is ideal to have critical members in specific roles within your core team. At a minimum, the team should include a director, an actor, an editor, a producer, and a director of photography (DP). The director leads the creative vision and guides the overall filmmaking process. The actor brings characters to life and plays a vital role in delivering compelling performances. The editor shapes the narrative and enhances the storytelling through meticulous editing. The producer ensures smooth scheduling, organization, and logistical aspects of the project. Finally, the DP is responsible for capturing the visual essence of your film through skilled cinematography. See also my Note on Assuming Multiple Roles further down, where you can take on editing and directing roles yourself.

Creating a Collaborative Environment

Assembling a core team is not just about finding individuals for specific roles. It's about building a fellowship of like-minded individuals who share your passion and dedication. Collaboration is the key to success in low-budget filmmaking. Each member brings unique skills and perspectives, contributing to the collective momentum of the project.

In filmmaking, lifetime collaborations among well-known individuals have led to remarkable cinematic achievements. For instance, the partnership between Martin Scorsese and actor Robert De Niro has produced iconic films like "Taxi Driver," "Raging Bull," "Goodfellas," and "The Irishman." Steven Spielberg, along with cinematographer Janusz Kamiński, has created visually stunning and emotionally impactful films such as "Schindler's List" and "Saving Private Ryan." Tim Burton and his frequent collaborator, actor Johnny Depp, have brought unique and visually striking movies like "Edward Scissorhands" to the screen. Christopher Nolan, together with cinematographer Hoyte van Hoytema, has delivered visually immersive and technically impressive cinematography in films such as "Interstellar" and "Dunkirk." The Coen brothers have jointly created critically acclaimed films like "Fargo" and "No Country for Old Men," collaborating with various talented actors. Quentin Tarantino's collaborations with cinematographer Robert Richardson have yielded memorable movies such as "Kill Bill" and "Once Upon a Time in Hollywood." These examples showcase the power of creative collaborations between directors and actors or directors and cinematographers in achieving extraordinary cinematic outcomes.

Managing Expectations and Realistic Planning

During meetings, it is vital to manage expectations and engage in realistic planning. As a DIY or low-budget filmmaker, you must work within your means and be resourceful. Evaluating the script and discussing what is feasible and realistic becomes crucial. You may discover hidden gems within your "friends'" personal networks that can contribute to your project. Perhaps someone's relative owns a restaurant where you can shoot a scene, or a grandparent has a farm that can serve as a unique location. Someone might have access to a cool car perfect for a character's transportation. By tapping into these networks, you can leverage existing resources and add depth to your production, all while fostering a sense of community and utilizing the strengths of your friends' connections.

Fostering Collaboration and Respect

During the Friend Phase, collaboration becomes paramount.

Assembling your core team is the first step, ideally including a director of photography, an actor, an editor, and a dedicated producer responsible for scheduling and organizing. If the director is not also an editor, including an editor in your core team is advisable, considering the challenges of scheduling and budget associated with that role. Respect and goodwill are essential, even when funds are limited. Consider hosting meetings at home and offering simple gestures like beverages and snacks or a meal. These small acts of kindness build positive momentum and strengthen the bond within your team, whereby even though you may not have the means to offer significant financial compensation, small gestures like a potluck dinner party of spaghetti and cheap wine can foster a positive and supportive environment. Taking inspiration from the approach of renowned filmmaker Francis Ford Coppola, who organized an informal dinner for the cast of "The Godfather," these gatherings can go beyond mere social events. By doing so, they could deepen their understanding of their roles and carry those experiences into their performances. This example showcases the power of immersive experiences and demonstrates how informal gatherings can contribute to a strong team dynamic and collaborative spirit. Like Coppola's dinner, treating your team members with respect and gratitude builds solid bonds and fuels creativity.

The Table Read and Making Realistic Plans

Within these regular meetings, one of your primary tasks is the reading of your script. This reading is a crucial step to make your project a tangible reality. As you prepare for the reading, you must cast roles, secure a location, and manage the necessary logistics. These initial steps foreshadow the challenges you will face in the production phase.

Logistics

A table read, also known as a script read-through, is a gathering of the film's cast and crew to read the screenplay aloud. It typically takes place during pre-production and serves as a crucial step in the filmmaking process. Regardless of the budget size, from zero-budget projects to multi-million dollar productions, table reads are considered a fundamental practice. They serve as a cost-effective tool that transcends budget limitations, offering an equalizing opportunity for projects of all scales to refine their storytelling.

Traditionally, you would assemble everyone in a physical space, such as a conference room or rehearsal studio, or even your regular meeting space. However, with the widespread use of video conferencing tools, virtual table reads have become increasingly common and accessible.

The benefits of a table read are numerous. First, it allows the cast and crew to familiarize themselves with the script, gaining a deeper understanding of the characters, story arcs, and overall tone. It provides an opportunity for the writer, director, and actors to assess the pacing, dialogue, and overall flow of the screenplay. Through the live reading, potential issues or areas for improvement can be identified early on, enabling collaborative discussions and revisions.

Table reads are invaluable in capturing the essence of the story, exploring character dynamics, and fine-tuning the dialogue. They offer a platform for you to gauge the effectiveness of your vision and make necessary adjustments before production begins. Additionally, table reads help build a sense of camaraderie among the cast and crew, fostering a collaborative and unified approach to the project.

The Power of Regular Meetings

Regular meetings are a powerful tool for collaboration and team management, particularly when financial resources are limited. While you may need a budget to invest, investing your time in meetings can have a significant impact on the momentum of your project. Here are a few reasons and examples highlighting the power of regular meetings.

Alignment and Vision: Regular meetings allow the team to align their visions and ensure everyone is on the same page. By discussing ideas, sharing insights, and clarifying goals, meetings foster a collective understanding of the project's direction and purpose.

Accountability and Progress Tracking: Meetings are checkpoints to review progress, discuss milestones, and set targets. By regularly checking in on tasks and responsibilities, team members can hold each other accountable and maintain a sense of progress and momentum.

Problem-Solving and Decision-Making: Meetings offer a platform for creative problem-solving and decision-making. By bringing together diverse perspectives, team members can brainstorm solutions, address challenges, and make informed decisions collectively.

Creative Collaboration: Regular meetings encourage creative collaboration among team members. By sharing ideas, exchanging feedback, and exploring different possibilities, meetings become a breeding ground for creativity, pushing the project forward.

Motivation and Support: Meetings provide an opportunity to celebrate achievements, share successes, and offer support. By recognizing individual and collective contributions, team members feel motivated and inspired to continue their efforts, fostering a positive and supportive environment.

One example of the power of regular meetings is the story of filmmaker Kevin Smith. When Smith made his breakout indie film "Clerks," he held regular meetings with his core team, discussing ideas, reviewing the script, and planning the production. These meetings not only helped in shaping the film but also built a strong bond among the team members, generating the momentum and dedication necessary to complete the project on a limited budget.

Another example is the renowned director Christopher Nolan, who emphasizes the importance of regular meetings with his production team. Nolan's approach involves meticulous planning and extensive discussions during pre-production meetings to ensure a shared understanding of the film's vision and technical requirements. These regular meetings enable his team to align their efforts, work within constraints, and bring his ambitious cinematic visions to life.

Regular meetings, even without a significant budget, are a vital component of the filmmaking process. By investing your time in planning, dreaming big, and discussing your project, you are laying the foundation for its realization. They can be the lifeblood of your project during the Friend Phase. By discussing ideas and plans openly, you transform mere thoughts into concrete actions. Collaborative conversations generate momentum and move your project closer to reality.

Assuming Multiple Roles

In DIY low micro-budget filmmaking, I recommend taking on the roles of the writer, director, and editor. By assuming these responsibilities, you have greater creative control and can entirely shape the narrative and visual storytelling of your film. This multi-faceted approach not only gives you creative autonomy but also allows for a cohesive and unified vision throughout the filmmaking process.

Additionally, it significantly reduces costs as you won't need to hire separate professionals for each position. Among these positions, the role of the editor tends to require the most time and can be a significant expense when hiring a professional editor. In a minimum-budget scenario, you might face limitations in finding an affordable editor or settle for someone with less experience or expertise. Furthermore, you may have to work around their availability, as they may take on other paid projects in between, potentially causing delays in the post-production process. By assuming the role of the editor yourself, you eliminate the need to hire and pay someone for this task. This not only saves money but also gives you complete control over the editing process and allows you to work at your own pace. You can devote time and attention to refining the film, ensuring it aligns with your artistic vision.

This level of control and cost-effectiveness empowers you to make the most of your limited budget and resources, maximizing the overall quality and impact of your film. Embracing these roles offers creative freedom and cost-effectiveness, making it a practical and strategic choice for aspiring low-micro-budget filmmakers.

The Friend Phase – Action Points

• Assemble your core team: Identify and recruit a director of photography, an actor, editor and a dedicated producer who will manage scheduling and organization.

• Schedule regular meetings: Set a consistent date, time, and location for team meetings to maintain communication, foster collaboration, and keep the project on track.

• Have a read-through of the script: a milestone that brings your project closer to reality.

• Assess script feasibility: Collaborate with your team to evaluate the practicality of your script within the constraints of your DIY, low-budget approach.

• Make necessary adjustments to ensure realistic execution.

• Discuss and manage expectations: Engage in open discussions with your collaborators to align on what is achievable within your budget and resources. Set realistic goals and plans for the upcoming phases of your project.

• As you complete these tasks, remember to maintain a collaborative and respectful atmosphere within your team.

• Embrace the power of regular meetings to build momentum and engage in meaningful discussions that will shape the direction of your project.

Anthony Ferraro

CHAPTER FOUR
THE FINANCE PHASE

Now that you've completed the readings, held meetings, and discussed your project, it's time to dive into the challenging and somewhat intimidating Finance Phase. This is the pivotal moment where you'll face the reality of budget constraints, but don't let it discourage you. Remember, even if you're working with a low or zero budget, there's always a way to bring your film to life. The primary goals of the Finance Phase are to:

- determine your budget
- explore funding options
- set a timeframe for raising the necessary funds

Physics 101 teaches us that the momentum of a moving object increases with mass and speed. We rely on this principle in the Finance Phase (just as we do in the *Momentum Budget* as a whole) to keep rolling forward. Overthinking or coming to a complete stop will hinder your progress. Instead, embrace the challenge and find ways to keep moving ahead.

When determining your budget, you'll likely turn to friends, family, and acquaintances for financial support. It's essential to manage your expectations and be resourceful. Remember, this approach applies even if you aim to raise a substantial amount, like $100,000 or more. Connections and networking play a significant role in finding the necessary funds. Utilize your personal network and explore potential avenues to secure financial backing.

Collaborate with your team to determine a realistic budget. Assess whether crowdfunding is a viable option. Your budget could range from a few hundred dollars to several thousand, so be honest and set a target that aligns with your financial resources.

Once you have determined your budget, you can start deciding how to allocate the funds. Prioritize essential elements, such as securing a location or involving a name actor for a brief but impactful role. These choices will shape your budget and help you maximize your available resources.

If the budget is limited, don't lose hope. Remember, you've already assembled a dedicated team and gone through extensive preparations. Even if challenges arise or a team member drops out, the momentum you've built and the support from your remaining collaborators will keep you moving forward. Stay on track, anticipate obstacles, and maintain your focus as you approach the final phase.

With shooting dates in sight, take a moment to breathe. Now, shift your attention toward post-production. Set clear deadlines for editing, sound design, and music composition. Establish milestones for each stage, such as completing the first and second drafts, and communicate them with your team. This clarity will ensure everyone is on the same page and striving towards completing your film.

As you embark on the Finance Phase, remember that challenges are part of the journey. Actors may drop out, locations may change, and unexpected hurdles may arise. However, your strong foundation and the team's collective momentum will help you overcome these obstacles. Stay committed, stick to your shooting dates, and move forward with the post-production process.

Keep your eyes on the prize—a finished film that reflects your vision and dedication. Look for suitable film festivals to aim for, as having a specific deadline can focus your efforts and drive your team toward completion. This final phase is the homestretch, where all the hard work pays off, and your film becomes a reality.

The Finance Phase may seem daunting, but it's integral to realizing your dreams. By embracing the challenge, managing your budget realistically, and maintaining the momentum you've built, you'll overcome financial constraints and bring your film to life. Stay focused, adapt to unexpected circumstances, and keep pushing forward as you enter this exciting chapter of your filmmaking journey.

Determining Your Budget Realities

Determining your budget is crucial in bringing your film project to life. It requires thoughtful consideration and creative problem-solving to work within your financial means. You need to be honest with yourself and your current finances when you choose an approach to determining your budget and finding the necessary resources to make your film a reality.

Pooling Resources with Friends

One option to consider is gathering your core team of friends and collectively contributing to the budget. For example, if you and four of your friends are passionate about the project, you could each forgo a weekend dinner or drinking outing and contribute $200, resulting in a $1,000 budget. This approach allows you to leverage the commitment and support of your close-knit team to make the film possible.

Approaching Investors

If you need a larger budget, consider approaching individuals with means who might be interested in investing in your film. Prepare a persuasive pitch highlighting your project's potential and its unique value proposition—approach known individuals who have expressed interest in the arts or have a history of supporting creative endeavors. For example, you could present the idea to someone for a $5,000 investment. Remember, effective networking and building relationships are key to finding potential investors.

Crowdfunding

Crowdfunding has become a popular option for filmmakers to raise project funds. Platforms like *Indiegogo, Kickstarter,* or *WeFunder* have allowed creators to connect with audiences and potential backers. While the crowdfunding platform landscape may evolve, they have proven track records at the time of this writing. A general rule of thumb is to gather your core team and compile a list of individuals you believe will support your cause. Multiply that number by $70 to estimate a potential crowdfunding revenue ballpark figure.

Personal Sacrifices

When determining your budget, it's essential to evaluate your personal priorities and assess how much you are willing to invest in your film. Consider what you might be willing to forgo to allocate funds toward your project. For instance, if you typically take a vacation with a budget of $3,000 to $5,000 at the end of the year, you could choose to forgo that trip and allocate the funds toward your film. Alternatively, you might delay purchasing a new vehicle and invest the money in your film instead. These personal sacrifices test your commitment and demonstrate your desire to make your film a reality.

Exploring your budget constraints involves thoughtfully evaluating available resources, employing innovative solutions, and applying creative problem-solving. Whether pooling resources with friends, seeking investment from individuals, exploring crowdfunding platforms, or making personal sacrifices, finding the financial means to make your film can be challenging but rewarding; remember, the cavalry is not coming to save the day. It's up to you and your team to take charge, be resourceful, and make your film a reality.

Embrace Low-Budget Filmmaking

In filmmaking, a limited budget should encourage aspiring filmmakers to pursue their creative visions. Embracing low-budget filmmaking can present unique opportunities for creative exploration and growth.

The Advantages of Low-Budget Filmmaking

Creative Exploration: Working with limited resources forces filmmakers to think creatively, finding innovative solutions to overcome budgetary limitations. This constraint can lead to unique storytelling approaches, unconventional visual styles, and inventive production techniques.

Focus on Storytelling: With fewer financial resources, emphasis can be placed on compelling narratives, strong characters, and engaging storytelling. A captivating story can capture an audience's attention regardless of production values, allowing filmmakers to shine through their storytelling abilities.

Freedom and Independence: Low-budget filmmaking often means fewer stakeholders and less external interference. Filmmakers have more control over their creative decisions, enabling them to stay true to their artistic vision.

Examples of Successful Low-Budget Filmmakers

Numerous accomplished filmmakers began their careers with low-budget projects, demonstrating that limited resources should not hinder success. Some notable examples include:

Robert Rodriguez

Rodriguez famously made his debut feature film "El Mariachi" with a budget of just $7,000. The film achieved critical acclaim and launched his career in Hollywood.

Kevin Smith

Smith financed his breakout film "Clerks" by maxing out credit cards and relying on favors from friends. The film's success propelled him to become a prominent independent filmmaker.

Christopher Nolan

Nolan's first feature film, "Following," was shot on a shoestring budget with a small crew and non-professional actors. The film garnered attention and was a steppingstone to his later blockbuster successes.

Maximizing Creativity on a Low Budget

Focus on Strong Characters and Storytelling: Invest time in developing compelling characters and crafting engaging narratives. A captivating story can compensate for production limitations and captivate audiences.

Utilize Available Resources: Identify locations, props, and equipment you can access for little or no cost. Make the most of the available resources, utilizing real-world settings and practical effects to enhance the authenticity of your film.

Embrace Natural Lighting: Natural lighting can add a unique aesthetic to your film while minimizing the need for expensive lighting equipment. Experiment with different times of day and locations to achieve visually stunning results.

Collaborate with a Talented Team: Surround yourself with a dedicated and passionate team who shares your vision. Maximize the talents and skills of your crew members, allowing them to contribute creatively and effectively.

Commit to the DIY Approach: Adopt a do-it-yourself mentality, taking on multiple roles and responsibilities as needed. By learning various aspects of filmmaking, you can reduce costs and maintain creative control.

Low-budget filmmaking should not be viewed as a limitation but as an opportunity for creative exploration and growth. Filmmakers can achieve compelling results regardless of financial constraints by focusing on storytelling, strong characters, engaging narratives and collaborating with a talented team. With a creative mindset and resourceful approach, low-budget filmmaking can pave the way for artistic expression and realizing your cinematic vision.

Budget Challenges and Maintaining Momentum

While low-budget filmmaking offers creative opportunities, countless potential roadblocks can hinder momentum. Establish a budget goal, make a plan, and remain committed to it. This section will provide motivation and guidance for overcoming financial obstacles and maintaining the momentum built in previous steps.

Budget Challenges and Roadblocks

Fear and Discomfort: Asking for financial support can be intimidating and uncomfortable, especially for first-time filmmakers. Overcoming this fear is crucial to move forward in acquiring the necessary funds.

Lack of Planning: Failing to devise a concrete plan for budget acquisition can lead to stagnation and the loss of momentum. Without a timeframe and clear objectives, progress can be hindered.

Rejection and Setbacks: Preparing for potential rejection or setbacks is essential when seeking financial support. Not everyone may be interested or able to contribute, but perseverance and resilience are key to success.

The "Put Up or Shut Up" Moment: Commitment and Determination: This phase separates the talk from the action. It requires a firm commitment and unwavering determination to pursue your budget goals. Stay focused, maintain motivation, and do not let setbacks discourage you.

Utilize Momentum: If you have built momentum in the previous steps of the momentum budget, use it as a driving force to propel you forward. The energy, enthusiasm, and progress achieved thus far should catalyze to overcome any financial obstacles.

Embrace Support and Collaboration: Reach out to potential supporters, such as friends, family, and acquaintances who may believe in your project. Share your passion and vision, and be willing to accept help and collaboration from others.

Maintaining Momentum and Moving Forward

Set a Timeframe: Establish a specific timeframe for budget acquisition. Give yourself a realistic deadline, whether it's 30 days or any other suitable period, to pursue and secure the necessary funds actively.

Stay Resilient: Be prepared to face challenges and setbacks along the way. Stay resilient, maintain a positive mindset, and remind yourself of your passion and commitment to making your film a reality.

Adapt and Adjust: If initial fundraising efforts fall short, be open to adjusting your plan and exploring alternative funding options, such as the aforementioned crowdfunding platforms like *Indiegogo* or *Kickstarter*. Adaptability is crucial in navigating the financial landscape.

Dreams vs Reality in Navigating DIY Film Finance

It's important not to overlook or downplay this truth: what you're truly doing is investing in yourself and the future of your creative team. Whether you're fresh out of school, self-taught, in the middle of your career, or approaching the twilight years of your life, at the beginning of this journey, you're essentially on your own. However, if you've been paying attention, you'll realize that you're not alone. You have your creative partners by your side.

Here's the honest truth:

DIY film finance is not about making money in any shape or form. It's about being resourceful and minimizing your expenses, allowing you to invest as little money as possible. This investment is not solely about money; it extends to your time and energy as well. You dedicate yourself to this craft, pouring your heart and soul into your projects. To be clear that it's not about magically acquiring large sums of money but about navigating this journey with the limited resources you can gather.

This guide is meant to empower you, regardless of your financial situation. It acknowledges the realities and challenges you may face, recognizing that every bit of investment, whether time, money, or both, matters. The intention is to help you explore strategies to make the most of the little resources you have, unlocking your creative potential and paving the way for a fulfilling filmmaking journey.

Embracing the Motivation to Prove Them Wrong

Have you ever sought advice from someone and received a sincere response advising you not to pursue your goal? They say, "My advice is not to try, do something else." Surprisingly, that may be the best advice you can receive. It implies that the path you're considering is challenging, and success may be unlikely. There are a few possible intentions behind such advice. First, it could stem from empathy, with the person wanting to spare you from the potential pain and struggle they foresee. Second, and more importantly, it could be a way to ignite your determination and provoke a response of, "I'll show you." When someone tells you not to do something, and you don't get discouraged but instead feel motivated to prove them wrong, it strongly indicates that you possess the resilience to endure the hardships of embarking on a difficult journey.

Storytelling Beyond Financial Constraints

In my filmmaking journey, I learned a valuable lesson about

finance: *the originality and resonance of your idea are paramount.* I embarked on a crowdfunding campaign for a project I was deeply passionate about, and through the support of others, I raised almost $40,000. With this funding, I brought my envisioned project to life, expecting it to be a breakthrough success. However, while the project performed well, and I achieved my vision without compromise, it didn't find the success I had hoped for.

It was then that I realized the power of simplicity and careful execution. For my next project, constrained by a limited budget, I had a simple yet compelling idea. I meticulously planned every aspect, from the cast to the crew to the story. With a budget of under $1,000, I created a film that surpassed all expectations. It became my most successful and talked-about project, accumulating over 3 million views across various platforms.

This experience taught me not to equate a large budget with a better project or a low budget with a worse one. Instead, *I understood the importance of focusing on the story itself.* By prioritizing the narrative, crafting engaging characters, and delivering a resonant message, you can create a remarkable film regardless of budgetary constraints. Ultimately, it is the story that captivates audiences and leaves a lasting impact.

The Finance Phase – Action Points

Navigating Budget Challenges and Maintaining Momentum:

- Overcome fear and discomfort in asking for financial support.

- Create a concrete plan and timeframe for budget acquisition.

- Prepare for potential rejection and setbacks.

- Stay committed and determined to pursue your budget goals.

- Utilize momentum from previous steps to propel you forward.

- Seek support and collaboration from friends and potential supporters.

- Stay resilient and maintain a positive mindset.

- Adapt and adjust your plan if needed.

- Explore alternative funding options, such as crowdfunding.

- Keep pushing forward and make your filmmaking dreams a reality.

Budget Acquisition:

- Establish a realistic budget goal.

- Overcome fear and discomfort in asking for financial support.

- Create a concrete plan and timeframe for budget acquisition.

- Prepare for potential rejection and setbacks.

- Stay committed and determined to pursue your budget goals.

- Utilize momentum to drive your progress.

- Seek collaboration with friends and potential supporters
  - Set a specific timeframe for budget acquisition.

- Stay resilient and maintain a positive mindset.

- Adapt and adjust your plan as necessary.

- Keep pushing forward and make your filmmaking dreams a reality.

Anthony Ferraro

CHAPTER FIVE
THE FINISH PHASE

In the final phase of the filmmaking journey, the focus is on scheduling and setting deadlines to bring all elements together and complete your project. To avoid last-minute derailments due to poor planning in post-production, it's essential to identify a film festival or streaming platform release that aligns with your project. Setting it as a goal will give your team a clear target to concentrate on, facilitating the completion of the post-production process within a defined timeline.

Challenges in Production and Post-Production

As you progress through the Finish Phase, it's important to acknowledge the challenges that may arise during production and post-production. Filmmaking rarely goes exactly as planned, and unexpected obstacles and changes are common. Embrace the reality that your production might deviate from the initial vision, and post-production may result in a different film than originally anticipated. Adaptability and flexibility are key to successfully navigating these challenges and ensuring the completion of a compelling final product.

Production Challenges

You will encounter unforeseen issues such as budget limitations, scheduling conflicts, technical difficulties, and weather conditions during production. These challenges can disrupt your plans and require you to think on your feet, make adjustments, and find creative solutions. Remember that the most critical aspect of production is capturing the essential elements of your story and characters, even if it means deviating from the original script or adjusting your vision to fit the circumstances.

Post-Production Changes

In post-production, the editing process can significantly shape the final film. It's common for editing choices, sound design, visual effects, and other post-production elements to result in a film that differs from the initial concept. Embrace the opportunity to refine and enhance your story during this phase. Stay open to new possibilities and trust the expertise of the post-production team you assembled during the Friends Phase. The ultimate goal is to create a cohesive and engaging final product that resonates with your audience.

Scheduling the Film Shoot

Embrace the Chaos! Scheduling and shooting a film can be an overwhelming yet exhilarating experience. It's the reward for all the hard work and momentum you've built throughout filmmaking. However, it's important to acknowledge the realities and challenges of the territory.

Film production is notorious for its unpredictability. Schedules will change, locations may fall through, and catering arrangements can go awry. Despite meticulous planning, unexpected hurdles will inevitably arise. Staying adaptable and approaching these obstacles with a problem-solving mindset is crucial.

When scheduling a no-budget production, it's essential to consider your budget constraints and determine which positions you can afford to pay. Identify the roles that are crucial but challenging to find volunteers for, such as DP (Director of Photography), sound, and lighting. These positions often require experienced individuals, so allocating a budget for them is important. Additionally, evaluate if you can afford other essential roles like makeup artists and script supervisors.

Unpaid positions should be chosen wisely. For example, having a motivated assistant director is valuable as they play a crucial role in keeping the production on schedule. While you can hire Production Assistants (PAs) inexpensively, it's essential to remember that they are not skilled crew members and should be utilized as extra hands to support the skilled team.

Properly feeding the crew is vital. While pizza may be an option, it should be considered a last resort. Providing nutritious meals is crucial for maintaining energy and morale on set. Neglecting to feed your team properly can have negative consequences for the overall production.

When selecting an assistant director, look for someone with a personality that will assertively keep the team and schedule on track. Their role is critical in maintaining organization and efficiency.

Rehearsing with the actors before the shoot day is highly recommended, especially on a tight budget. This helps streamline discussions about character and motivation, allowing more efficient use of time and resources on the actual shooting day.

Lastly, remember to have fun. Filmmaking is an exciting and enjoyable process. Ensuring a positive and enjoyable atmosphere on set will foster a collaborative and motivated crew. Treating people respectfully and maintaining a good attitude will encourage crew members to work with you again, creating a more stable and productive team for future projects.

These suggestions are based on general advice and standard practices in no-budget productions. It's essential to adapt them to your specific circumstances and resources. Online resources and filmmaking communities can provide further insights and tips for scheduling a successful no-budget production.

You Will Underestimate Post-Production

Post-production is a critical phase of filmmaking that can significantly shape the final outcome of your film. Recognizing that the editing process may change your original vision is important. The editor's role is paramount, spending the most time with the project and bringing a fresh perspective that can fix mistakes made during shooting or reveal story problems that were previously unnoticed.

If this is your first film, one valuable piece of advice is to learn to do the editing yourself. Developing editing skills can save you time and money and serve you throughout your filmmaking career. As discussed in previous phase sections, DIY filmmaking often requires wearing multiple hats, and being an editor adds an unshakable aspect to your skillset. Learning to edit allows you to have creative control over the narrative and enhances your understanding of the filmmaking process.

Sound design and mixing are equally crucial aspects of post-production. The film is a visual medium, but good sound can elevate a lackluster moment, while bad sound can diminish the impact of a visually striking scene. Refrain from skimming on sound design; invest time and resources to ensure the audio elements enhance the viewing experience. If you're following my post-Dogma 95 advice from the introduction, please be aware that unlike natural practical lighting, proper recording of dialogue is essential.

If you're working on a genre film or have visual effects in your project, it's essential to pay attention to their demands. First, consider the budget limitations as visual effects can be expensive. Second, be prepared for the time it takes to complete visual effects shots, even with a friendly rate. When working with limited resources, a short four-second visual effects shot can take up to a month. Professional visual effects work can be cost-prohibitive, often exceeding the entire budget of your film. It's crucial to understand what you can afford and the time it will take to deliver high-quality visual effects.

If you cannot edit yourself, having an editor as part of your core team early on is highly beneficial. Their expertise will ensure a smooth and efficient post-production process. Similarly, if you plan to hire an editor and a visual effects artist, remember that their services may exceed your budget limitations. As in Phase 2, finding individuals willing to work for a belief in the project may result in longer turnaround times than anticipated.

It's essential to know that many films never leave the post-production phase. Challenges can arise, both creative and logistical, that can stall or halt the process altogether. However, regardless of your difficulties, embrace the start of your journey and seize the opportunity to learn one of the key post-production skills.

While it's important to maintain a can-do attitude and embrace the joy and excitement of planning, creation, and being on set, it would be remiss to overlook the significance of having a solid post-production plan. Post-production is the make-or-break phase, where the final touches are added to your film. It's a time that requires careful attention, meticulous organization, and unwavering dedication. Take a moment to digest the importance of post-production and its impact on your film's overall success. By prioritizing and investing in this crucial phase, you increase the chances of creating a polished and impactful final product.

Submission Deadlines As Motivation

To keep the project on track, establish deadlines and milestones for each stage of the production process. In addition to traditional film festivals, consider the option of releasing your film on a streaming platform. Many platforms serve as hubs with a large following, offering an opportunity to reach a broader audience. By targeting these platforms, you can maximize exposure and gain more viewers than through a traditional festival run alone.

The Importance of Eyeballs and Reaching a Wide Audience

While film festivals are a traditional avenue for showcasing films, streaming platforms offer an alternative route to reach a large number of viewers. The goal is to have your film seen by as many people as possible. Releasing a film on a streaming platform with a modest budget may attract significantly more viewers than a well funded film that solely relies on festival screenings. As you consider the potential impact of reaching millions of viewers through streaming platforms, keep in mind that film festivals offer unique value and benefits to your filmmaking journey.

Understanding the Impact of Streaming Platforms

Streaming platforms have revolutionized the film industry by providing access to a global audience. They offer a convenient and cost-effective way to distribute and showcase films. While traditional film festivals still hold value, exploring streaming platforms as a release option can be an effective strategy to gain visibility and generate buzz around your project.

Considering Expenses in Reaching That Larger Audience

Submitting films to festivals can be costly, so it's crucial to research attendance records, community outreach, and peer reviews to make an informed choice. Expanding your focus to streaming platforms can reduce these costs while reaching a wider audience. This broader reach allows your film to be discovered by individuals who may have yet to attend festivals or have access to your work otherwise.

The value of Film Festivals

Watching your film in the dark with a roomful of strangers can be humbling and exhilarating. It is a unique experience that allows you to witness the impact of your work on an audience, and it can be a transformative moment in your filmmaking journey. Let's take a moment to explore the significance of this experience and delve into the power of film festivals as invaluable community builders and objective sounding boards for the quality of your work.

Let's discuss the value of taking your movie out into the world, including the opportunities it provides for meeting other creatives, networking with potential investors, and finding inspiration or challenges for your next project.

Attending film festivals in person is a vital part of your filmmaking journey, despite the associated costs. It's essential to choose festivals wisely, and utilizing peer review sites can help make informed decisions. If your work isn't accepted, don't be disheartened, as the selection process can be subjective. Keep moving forward and maintain a positive attitude. Additionally, it's worth building relationships with festival programmers and organizers, as it can open doors within the industry.

Film Festivals as Community Builders

Film festivals are crucial in building a supportive and vibrant filmmaking community. They bring together filmmakers, industry professionals, and film enthusiasts worldwide. These events provide opportunities for networking, collaboration, and exposure to a wider audience. Participating in film festivals makes you part of a community that shares your passion for cinema. You can exchange ideas, gain insights from fellow filmmakers, and forge valuable connections to elevate your career.

Film festivals also serve as objective sounding boards for the quality of your work. The feedback and reactions you receive from audiences and industry professionals can be invaluable in assessing the strengths and weaknesses of your film. Constructive criticism and honest assessments can guide you in refining your storytelling techniques, enhancing technical aspects, or exploring new creative directions. Through this feedback loop, you can grow as a filmmaker and continue to improve your craft.

While streaming platforms may provide feedback on your film, it's important to note that the feedback received there may only sometimes be helpful or constructive. Often, you'll encounter two extremes: either overly positive comments that offer little critical evaluation or harsh and thoughtless negative comments. These extremes contribute little to your creative journey or help you grow as a filmmaker. Remember that, while feedback is important for growth, it's crucial to be selective about the sources and prioritize feedback that is constructive, thoughtful, and aligned with your artistic vision.

Echoing the successful approach of phase 2, building a network of trusted peers, mentors, or industry professionals who can provide thoughtful feedback can be immensely beneficial. Collaborating with other filmmakers, joining filmmaking communities, or seeking feedback from reputable film organizations can help you gather valuable insights and constructive criticism that will aid in your growth as a filmmaker.

Embracing the Dissatisfaction

At the end of the Finish Phase, we reach a crucial realization: The very Last Step is the First Step of the next project. Completing your film is a significant accomplishment, but it's essential to acknowledge that it may fail to meet your expectations, especially if it's your first project. The truth may be harsh, but it's a reality for many aspiring filmmakers. If one thousand individuals read this guide, it's possible that among us, one born talent will create an exceptional film and launch a successful career right out of the gate. However, filmmaking is a continuous journey of growth and improvement for the remaining nine hundred and ninety-nine of us.

It's crucial to avoid fixating on any perceived limitations of your completed film and, instead, channel that energy into initiating your next project. To quote Martha Graham,

"There is no satisfaction whatever at any time. There is only a queer, divine dissatisfaction, a blessed unrest that keeps us marching and makes 'us' MORE alive than the others."

This divine dissatisfaction fuels our desire to improve, learn, and push ourselves creatively continually.

Be sure to complete your film before you embark on your next one. Use the lessons learned from your previous project as a foundation for growth. Embrace the opportunity to evolve as a filmmaker and apply newfound knowledge and skills to your next endeavor. Each project brings valuable experience, allowing you to refine your craft and move closer to realizing your artistic vision.

Remember, a filmmaker's journey is a continuous process of learning, creating, and improving. Embrace the blessed unrest within you and stay committed to growth and creative exploration. As you begin your next project, let the dissatisfaction drive you, making you more attuned to the nuances of your craft. Stay inspired, stay hungry, and continue pursuing your filmmaking dreams.

The Finish Phase – Action Points

- Set clear deadlines and milestones for each stage of the production process.

- Identify a film festival or streaming platform release that aligns with your project and use it as a goal to aim for.

- Embrace the challenges of production and post-production and adapt to unexpected changes.

- Stay organized and flexible during the shoot, as schedules, locations, and catering arrangements may change.

- Understand that the editing process may alter your original vision and be open to refining and enhancing your story.

- Consider learning to edit yourself to save time and money and have creative control over your film.

- Give importance to sound design and mixing to enhance the overall viewing experience.

- Be aware of the potential costs and time requirements of visual effects, and manage your expectations accordingly.

- If unable to edit yourself, consider having an editor as part of your core team.

- Keep in mind that post-production can be a challenging phase, and having a solid plan is essential for success.

• Embrace the dissatisfaction that drives you to continually improve and start planning your next project without dwelling on the shortcomings of your finished film.

• View each project as a steppingstone in your journey as a filmmaker and use the lessons learned to grow and evolve creatively.

Anthony Ferraro

CONCLUSION

Let's take a moment to reflect on the phases we've explored and reaffirm the fundamental principles we've discussed throughout. The Four F's—Free, Friends, Finance, and Finish—have provided a solid framework to guide you on your filmmaking path. Understanding the realities of DIY Filmmaking is crucial; it's not merely a coupon code for shortcuts, but a symbol of the dedication and hard work required to bring your vision to life. As we conclude this guide, I want to leave you with some final thoughts to reflect on. For aspiring and struggling filmmakers, this is a very simple and straightforward roadmap to navigate and overcome the roadblocks and gatekeepers that may stand in your way. Embrace the DIY mentality, fuel your passion, and step into the world of filmmaking with confidence and purpose.

Embracing Momentum and Looking Ahead

By embracing the momentum of resourcefulness, resilience, and collaboration, filmmakers can navigate obstacles and pave a path to success with grit and determination. The aim of this book is to emphasize the significance of looking ahead, having a clear purpose, and maintaining unwavering determination, all supported by the right mindset and a collaborative team. The future of bringing your original ideas to life rests within your grasp, and this book encourages you to seize creative autonomy and forge ahead fearlessly.

The Reality of DIY Filmmaking

One of the essential aspects we emphasized in this guide is the concept of DIY filmmaking. However, it's crucial to clarify that DIY doesn't mean doing everything for free. Instead, it means taking charge of your filmmaking journey 'Yourself" and actively participating in various aspects. Recognize that your time and dedication have a tangible value, equivalent to hundreds of thousands of dollars of your own time and unpaid sweat equity. By embracing the DIY mindset, you empower yourself to be a proactive creator and take ownership of your vision.

Maintaining Momentum and Taking Action

Throughout this guide, I've stressed the significance of maintaining momentum. Momentum is the lifeblood of any creative endeavor, propelling you forward and driving your progress. It's crucial to embrace action as it begets further action. Instead of resisting or succumbing to obstacles, put your head down, wrap your arms around your team, and move forward. Momentum creates a sense of purpose, fuels your passion, and keeps your dreams alive.

Building Filmmaking Connections for Success

Building your community is paramount in the filmmaking journey. One of the most effective ways to align yourself with talented and essential individuals in filmmaking is to collaborate with them before they achieve widespread recognition. By working together early, you can establish meaningful connections and foster relationships that grow and flourish as your careers progress. Embrace the opportunity to collaborate with emerging talents as they bring fresh perspectives, innovative ideas, and a shared passion for creating impactful films. Remember, the bonds you form today can shape the trajectory of your future filmmaking endeavors, so invest in building a supportive and interconnected community.

Understanding the Last Step as the Next First Step

As filmmakers, we often find ourselves consumed by the completion of a project. However, it's vital to recognize that the end of one film marks the beginning of the next. The last step in your current project becomes the first step of your next one. Embrace this concept and use the lessons learned, the challenges, and the victories to fuel your growth and evolution as a filmmaker.

Final Words of Encouragement

Filmmaking is a demanding and challenging pursuit, but it is also a remarkable and rewarding journey of self-discovery, creative expression, and storytelling. Embrace the dissatisfaction within you, for it is the driving force that propels you to improve and grow as a filmmaker continually. Trust in your vision, believe in your abilities, and surround yourself with a dedicated and passionate team who shares your dreams.

Remember, filmmaking is an ongoing process of learning, creating, and pushing boundaries. It requires determination, resilience, and the willingness to adapt and evolve. Embrace the opportunities and challenges that come your way, they are the catalysts for growth and innovation. Cherish every moment, both the triumphs and the setbacks, as they shape you as an artist and define your unique voice.

I invite you to take these words to heart and embark on your filmmaking journey with passion, determination, and an unwavering commitment to your craft. Stay true to yourself, trust your instincts, and never lose sight of your dreams. The world awaits your stories, your vision, and your unique perspective. Harness the momentum, move forward confidently, and let your passion for filmmaking guide you toward turning your ideas into reality.

The Outsider Filmmaker

Anthony Ferraro

Bio

Anthony R. Ferraro, a self-taught filmmaker, spent the past two decades fully immersed in independent cinema, directing feature films, shorts, and web series. His sci-fi film "Aeranger" earned millions of views, establishing him as an accomplished storyteller. Anthony's practical knowledge forms the foundation for everything he shares on his popular YouTube channel, Create Sci-Fi, with over 3 million views. In "The Outsider Filmmaker: Start Your Film Without Funding," Anthony wholeheartedly shares practical, straightforward suggestions based on everyday logic and understanding, empowering aspiring filmmakers to embrace their creative aspirations and take the leap into the world of filmmaking.

Explore all of Anthony's films, channel links, news, store, and social media connections at:
www.ferrarofilm.com

Made in USA - North Chelmsford, MA
1384629_9798218262976
09.20.2023 1526